GRAPHIC TALES OF THE SUPERNATURAL

WEREWOLVES

TORIES OF DEADLY SHAPE-SHIFTERS

written and illustrated by

Gary Jeffrey

New York

Published in 2011 by The Rosen Publishing Group, Inc.
29 East 21st Street, New York, NY 10010

First edition

Designed and produced by
David West Books

Photo credits:
p4l, Dennis from Atlanta; p6t, lrargerich; p7tl, Bohringer

Library of Congress Cataloging-in-Publication Data

Jeffrey, Gary.
Werewolves : stories of deadly shape-shifters / Gary Jeffrey.
    p. cm. -- (Graphic tales of the supernatural)
Includes bibliographical references and index.
ISBN 978-1-4488-1901-0 (library binding) -- ISBN 978-1-4488-1911-9
(pbk.) -- ISBN 978-1-4488-1912-6 (6-pack)
1. Werewolves--Comic books, strips, etc. I. Title.
GR830.W4J44 2011
398.24'54--dc22

        2010027644

Manufactured in China

CPSIA Compliance Information: Batch #DW1102YA:
For further information contact Rosen Publishing, New York, New York, at 1-800-237-9932.

CONTENTS

SHADOW OF THE WOLF

A werewolf is a person who shape-shifts into the form of a wolflike creature. The idea of this terrifying transformation originated in the myth and folklore of many European regions.

CANIS LUPUS

Swift, cunning, savage, and boldly ferocious when cornered, wolves have long been feared and admired by their human hunter rivals. Stories of humans transforming into wolves date from ancient times right up to the modern era. The wolf, a creature of the night, seemed to express the dark-hearted cruelty that lurked in man. Longtime scavengers of battlefields, wolves are also linked with death.

In Greek mythology, Lycaon was turned into a werewolf by Zeus, after offering the god human flesh.

A gray wolf

A werewolf gargoyle on Notre Dame cathedral, in Paris, France

TOOTH AND CLAW

In Iceland, a werewolf is called *varulfur*; in Italy, a *lupo mannero*, and in France, a *loup-garou*. France and Germany were plagued by werewolf killings for more than 200 years. One of the most famous is the Beast of Gevaudan (see page 16).

Was the wolf of Chazes the Beast of Gevaudan?

4

WEREWOLF TYPES

In traditional folklore, werewolves are people who completely transform into large and very nasty wolves. The modern notion of a werewolf is a horrifying half-man, half-beast. Both kinds of werewolves share an unrestrained desire to kill and maim—an unleashing of the beast within.

Some werewolves are credited with supernatural powers and are believed to be in league with the devil. Accompanied by a foul odor, they are capable of bewitching people—and worse!

Modern versions of werewolves have been influenced by horror fiction and movies. No longer merely a wolf, the werewolf is now a hideous monster that walks upright.

WEREWOLF LORE

Some people become werewolves after being cursed by witches. Others are infected with lycanthropy by being bitten or scratched by a werewolf, and some are just born with it.

TRANSFORMATIONS

The change into a wolf can be triggered by putting on an entire wolfskin or a simple belt made of wolf's fur. Other ways include drinking from the puddle collected in a wolf's footprint or using a special ointment made from bat's blood or nightshade (a poisonous plant).

It was once thought sleepir outdoors during a fu moon, or being born under full moon, could tur people into werewolve

A werewolf may spend many hours or even days in wolf form.

Excessive facial hair was thought to be a sign someone was actually a werewolf.

SHAPE-SHIFTERS

People who have become werewolves are believed to exhibit tell-tale signs, such as pale, rough skin, and bushy eyebrows that mee in the middle. They may have excessive hair on their faces, hands, and feet. According to one theory, werewolves wear their wolf skin with the fur on the inside when assuming human form.

ROTECTION

Werewolves can be
repelled by iron and silver.
Objects made from these
metals thrown over a
werewolf's head will stop
it in its tracks, as will
scalding a werewolf
with boiling water.

*Failure to ward off werewolves
successfully can have dire
consequences for forest dwellers.*

*The poisonous herb Anconitum,
or Wolfsbane, has been used
through the ages as a werewolf
repellant. It was also
believed to cause
lycanthropy if eaten.*

*The idea that silver bullets
could kill werewolves
originated in the 18th century.*

SLAYING THE BEAST WITHIN

According to ancient myth, werewolves
could be cured if they were kept moving
until exhausted. In the Middle Ages, it was
believed that calling werewolves by their
Christian name three times, or hitting them
on the head three times with a metal knife,
could cure them.

Cures should be tried since werewolves
can only be killed with silver projectiles, or
by inflicting heart or brain damage. They
return to human form before death.

*In medieval
times, a person
found guilty of
being a
werewolf often
met with a
brutal end.*

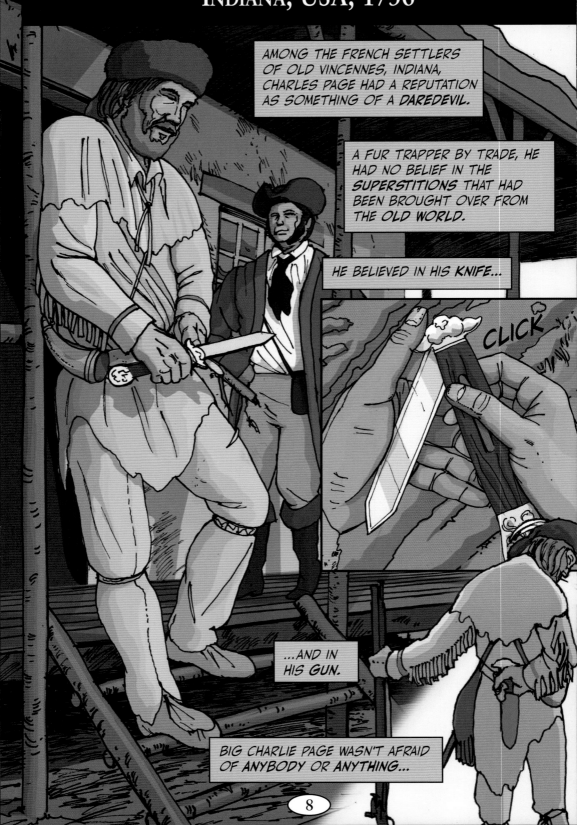

CURSE OF THE WEREWOLF
INDIANA, USA, 1736

AMONG THE FRENCH SETTLERS OF OLD VINCENNES, INDIANA, CHARLES PAGE HAD A REPUTATION AS SOMETHING OF A *DAREDEVIL*.

A FUR TRAPPER BY TRADE, HE HAD NO BELIEF IN THE *SUPERSTITIONS* THAT HAD BEEN BROUGHT OVER FROM THE OLD WORLD.

HE BELIEVED IN HIS *KNIFE*...

CLICK

...AND IN HIS GUN.

BIG CHARLIE PAGE WASN'T AFRAID OF ANYBODY OR ANYTHING...

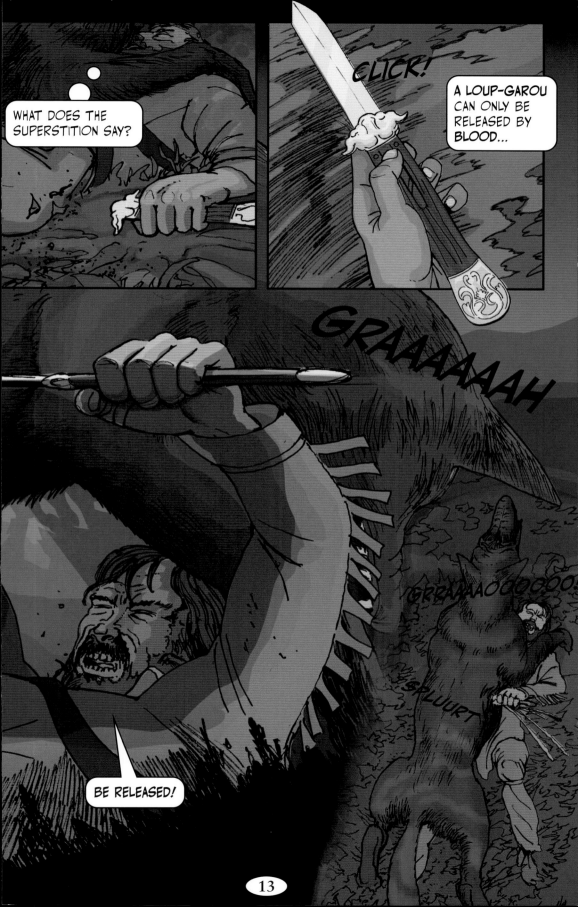

HUH? IT'S CHANGING!

THE ANIMAL'S WEIGHT—IT'S GETTING *LIGHTER*...

AS IT BECAME HUMAN, PAGE RECOGNIZED HIS BEST FRIEND, JEAN VATEL.

J—JEAN, IS THAT YOU?

HERE, PUT THIS ON.

EACH NIGHT VATEL HAD **TRANSFORMED** AND ROAMED THE COUNTRYSIDE TO SATISFY HIS **CRAVINGS.**

GRRRRAAAGH!

PAGE HADN'T SEEN VATEL FOR WEEKS. HE HAD BEEN SICK WITH A FEVER. BUT UNKNOWN TO EVERYONE, HE WAS REALLY SICK FROM **BEWITCHMENT.**

SICKENED BY HIS SECRET HE HAD SOUGHT OUT HIS FRIEND, KNOWING THAT THE CURSE COULD ONLY BE BROKEN BY **BLOOD.**

VATEL VOWED NEVER TO STRAY AGAIN.

THE END

THE BEAST OF GEVAUDAN
NORTHERN FRANCE, 1765

SEPTEMBER 21, 1765, POMMIER WOODS, SAINTE-MARIE-DES-CHAZES. A WOLF HUNT WAS IN PROGRESS...

THE SHOUT'S GONE UP—IT'S COMING OUT!

RINCHARD, SHOULDER YOUR WEAPON—WE MUST BE READY!

ANTOINE DE BEAUTERNE, THE KING'S CHIEF HUNSTMAN, HAD BEEN TRACKING THE ANIMAL SINCE JUNE.

THERE IT IS!

THE MORBACH MONSTER
SOUTHEASTERN GERMANY, 1988

US ARMY **SECURITY POLICE** WERE IN **WENIGERATH,** GERMANY, HEADED TO THE MORBACH MUNITIONS DUMP, WHEN THE DRIVER **NOTICED** SOMETHING...

HEY, LOOK! THE CANDLE'S OUT IN THE VILLAGE SHRINE.

THE SHRINE WAS SOMETIMES LIT TO **PROTECT** THE VILLAGE.

AND IT'S A FULL MOON!

UH-OH, YOU KNOW WHAT THAT MEANS! *WOOOOOO* —THE WEREWOLF'S GOING TO BE OUT TONIGHT!

THE WEREWOLF —YEAH, RIGHT!

ALTHOUGH HE WAS FAIRLY *NEW* ON THE BASE, LUKE HAD HEARD THE STORY—EVERYONE HAD. IT WAS A WELL-KNOWN PIECE OF VILLAGE *FOLKLORE*.

BACK IN *1812*, THOMAS SCHWYTZER, A *DESERTER* FROM NAPOLEON'S RUSSIAN CAMPAIGN, WAS MAKING HIS WAY BACK TO HIS *HOMELAND* IN NORTHERN FRANCE *WHEN...*

HEY, A FARMHOUSE! COME ON, THEY MIGHT HAVE FOOD.

DESERTED!

WHAT ELSE IS THERE?

BANG

GRNNAGH!

HEY, WHAT ARE YOU DOING?

GET THEM!

DURING THE STRUGGLE, THE FARMER AND HIS BOY ARE **KILLED**...

AAAAGH!

BANG!

AIEEEEEEEE!

BUT A **CHANGE** COMES OVER SCHWYTZER. EVEN THE **BRIGANDS** HE IS TRAVELING WITH ARE **APPALLED**...

HE ROBS AND KILLS AT WILL!

I AGREE—HE'S **OUT** OF CONTROL. IT'LL BE US **NEXT**.

SHUNNED BY HIS COMPANIONS, SCHWYTZER RETREATS **DEEPER** INTO THE **FOREST**.

IN THE AREA WHERE HE IS **CAMPED**, CATTLE ARE FOUND **KILLED** AND **MUTILATED**...

...AS IF BY AN **ENORMOUS** ANIMAL.

GKKKKKRRROOUGH

MOVING IN, THE VILLAGERS DISCOVER SCHWYTZER...
HE IS THE WOLF! KILL HIM!
AAAAGH!
SCHWYTZER IS BURIED AT THE CROSSROADS. A SHRINE IS ERECTED.
DURING EVERY FULL MOON, WE MUST KEEP THIS CANDLE LIT...
...OR THE WEREWOLF WILL RETURN.

MORE WEREWOLF STORIES

The last ever werewolf trial and execution happened in 1720, marking the end of widespread belief in lycanthropy. However, hair-raising stories from this dark era of history remain to haunt the human imagination....

This print shows the fear that wolves inspired in medieval folk

WEREWOLF OF BEDBURG, 1589

Bedburg, near Cologne, in Germany, had one of the most famous werewolf trials in history. A wealthy farmer, widower Peter Stubbe, was arrested. After being stretched on the rack, he confessed to having practiced black magic since he was twelve. He claimed the Devil gave him a magical belt, which enabled him to change into "the likeness of a greedy, devouring wolf, with most sharp and cruel teeth, a huge body, and mighty paws." He admitted to killing at least 16 people over 25 years. His execution was one of the most brutal ever recorded. Stubbe was tied to a wagon wheel and had parts of his flesh torn off with red hot pincers. Then his limbs were broken through the spokes, and he was beheaded and burnt.

Stubbe causes carnage.

HANS THE WEREWOLF, 1651

Estonia in Eastern Europe had the unusual tradition of trying witches and werewolves together. This was how, at a witch trial, an 18-year-old boy called Hans came to confess to the court that he was in fact a werewolf.

ans said he had been given the power of transformation by a
ysterious man in black, and had hunted as a werewolf for two
ears. Asked if his body took part in the hunt, or if only his
oul was altered, Hans confirmed that he had found a dog's
eeth-marks on his own leg, which he had received while a
erewolf. Further asked whether he felt himself to be a man or
beast while transformed, he said that he felt himself to be a
east. Hans was duly burnt as a witch.

WOLF OF ANSBACH, 1685

his is the strange case of a werewolf seemingly possessed by
e spirit of a ghost. The Principality of Ansbach (in modern-
ay Bavaria, Germany) came under attack by a particularly
avage lone wolf.

At first merely attacking livestock, the wolf soon moved on to
unting women and children. The townspeople thought the
olf was possessed by their cruel, recently deceased mayor.
hey hunted the wolf with dogs, driving it from a forest lair out
to the open. It jumped in an open well to escape, but was
en slain inside the well.

The body was removed and, once the muzzle had been cut
ff, dressed in the likeness of the dead mayor. The villagers
ragged the wolf in mayor's clothing through the streets and
ung it from a gallows. Finally, the body was taken down and
reserved for display in a local museum.

The fate of the Ansbach wolf

GLOSSARY

apprehensive Fearing future trouble or evil.
brigand A bandit or robber.
Canis lupus The scientific name for wolves.
carcass The dead body of an animal.
deliverance The act of being saved.
deserter Someone who runs away from duty with no plan to return.
diabolical Devilish, outrageously wicked.
forbade Commanded not to do something.
gallows A wooden frame from which condemned people were executed by hanging.
gargoyle A grotesquely carved figure of a human or animal.
girdle A belt, cord, or sash.
infected Invaded by a disease-carrying virus or bacterium.
innkeeper A person who owns or manages an inn or a hotel.
lycanthropy The condition of being a werewolf.
mangy Shabby or worn.
marquis A ruler of a border area.
maul To injure by a rough beating.
mutilated Injured or disfigured.
nape The back of the neck.
odor A smell, especially a bad one.
ointment A medicine applied to the skin.
possess To control from within.
potion A drink, especially one said to have medical properties or magical powers.
rabid Furious or raging.
scald To burn with hot liquid or steam.
scavenger An animal that feeds on dead organic matter.
shape-shift To change forms.
shrapnel A hollow projectile designed to explode before reaching the target, letting loose sharp metallic particles.
shrine A place made holy by its history or association.
shun To keep away from.
sulfur An element that burns with a suffocating odor.
terrorize To produce widespread fear by surprise acts of violence.
vow A solemn promise.

FOR MORE INFORMATION

ORGANIZATIONS

Shapeshifter Emporium
http://www.lycanthropes.org/shapeshifter/sser-emp.htm

FOR FURTHER READING

Baring-Gould, Sabine. *The Book of Were-Wolves*. Scotts Valley, CA: CreateSpace, 2010.

Barnhill, Kelly Regan. *Blood-Sucking, Man-Eating Monsters*. Mankato, MN: Capstone Press, 2009.

Curran, Bob. *Werewolves: A Field Guide to Shapeshifters, Lycanthropes, and Man-Beasts*. Franklin Lakes, NJ: New Page Books, 2009.

Godfrey, Linda S. *Hunting the American Werewolf*. Black Earth, WI: Trails Media Group, 2006.

Godfrey, Linda S. *Werewolves* (Mysteries, Legends, and Unexplained Phenomena). New York, NY: Checkmark Books, 2008.

Whiting, Jim. *Scary Monsters*. Mankato, MN: Capstone Publishing, 2010.

INDEX

A
Ansbach, 45

B
Bavaria, 45
Bedburg, 44
Besseyre-Saint-Mary, La, 25
brigand, 36, 46

C
Canis lupus, 4, 46
carcass, 20, 46
Chazes, 4, 16, 20

D
deserter, 33, 46
diabolical, 23, 46

G
gallows, 45, 46
gargoyle, 4, 46
Gevaudan, 4, 16
girdle, 23, 46

I
infected, 6, 46
innkeeper, 19, 46

L
loup-garou, 4
Lozere, 20, 22
lupo mannero, 4

L
lycanthropy, 6, 7, 44, 46
Lycaon, 4

M
mangy, 19, 46
marquis, 27, 31, 46
maul, 19, 46
Morbach, 37
mutilate, 36, 46

N
nape, 29, 46
Napolean, 33
nightshade, 6
Notre Dame, 4

O
odor, 5, 46
ointment, 6, 46

P
Paulhac, 21
possess, 45, 46
potion, 23, 46

R
rabid, 35, 46

S
scald, 7, 46
scavenger, 4, 46
Schwytzer, Thomas, 32, 36, 38

shape-shift, 4, 6, 46
shrapnel, 17, 46
shrine, 32, 38, 43, 46
shun, 36, 46
Stubbe, Peter, 44
sulfur, 12, 46

T
terrorize, 19, 46

V
varulfur, 4
vow, 15, 46

W
Wenigerath, Germany, 32

Z
Zeus, 4

Web Sites

Due to the changing nature of Internet links, Rosen Publishing has developed an online list of Web sites related to the subject of this book. This site is updated regularly. Please use this link to access the list:

http://www.rosenlinks.com/gts/were